CD
Aeòlus!

Earrann I

Earrann II

Earrann III

Earrann IV

Other books edited and translated by Bill Innes:

Chì Mi: The Gaelic Poetry of Donald John Macdonald, 2001

Fo Sgàil a' Swastika: Under the Shadow of the Swastika,
Dòmhnall Iain MacDhòmhnaill 2000

Old South Uist with Eriskay and Benbecula, 2006

St Valery: The Impossible Odds, 2007

Aeòlus!

Donald Macintyre
1889 — 1964

Aeòlus!

Donald Macintyre

Translated by
Bill Innes

Grace Note
Publications

English Translation of Aeòlus!
first Published in Great Britain in 2008 by
Grace Note Publications Ltd
Grange of Locherlour
Ochtertyre
Perthshire PH7 4JS
Scotland
books@gracenotereading.co.uk

ISBN : 978-0-9552326-2-6

The poem was first published as *Aeòlus agus am Balg* in *Sporan Dhòmhnaill:*
Gaelic Poems and Songs by the late Donald Macintyre
by Scottish Academic Press for the Gaelic Texts Society Edinburgh, 1968

Original Concept and reading of the poem: Bill Innes
CD Production: Sandy Stanage
© 2008 Music composed and performed by Sandy Stanage.

Drawings by Merrill McWilliam

Photographs © 2008 Estate of Donald Macintyre
unless otherwise stated

Chuidich Urras Brosnachaidh na Gàidhlig le cosgaisean an leabhair

The publisher acknowledges assistance from The Gaelic Language Promotion
Trust towards the cost of publication

British Library Cataloguing-in-Publications Data
A catalogue record for this book is available from the British Library

Printed and bound in Great Britain by Biddles Ltd, King's Lynn, Norfolk

Dedication

Tha an leabhar seo na chuimhneachan air còignear à aon teaghlach a
chaill am beatha ann an tubaist chianail nuair a bhuail stoirm mhòr
Uibhist air an 11mh latha dhen Fhaoilleach, 2005

This book is dedicated to the memory of five members of a South Uist
family who so tragically lost their lives in a great storm which struck
the island on January 11th, 2005.

Archie and Murdina Macpherson

Their children
Andrew John Macpherson (age 7)
Hannah Macpherson (age 5)

Murdina's father
Calum Campbell

Contents

Aeòlus!

Earrann I

Earrann II

Earrann III

Earrann IV

Acknowledgements

The poetry of Donald Macintyre has been an inspiration and joy to me since his collected works were published in 1968. The wonderfully musical flow of his verse seems to spring naturally from the idiomatic Gaelic spoken by the old people of my childhood. It is a joy to recite or sing and needs to be read with lips moving as one savours the sounds! Yet his poetry complies effortlessly with the intricate rules of ancient metres.

There are many people to be thanked. It has been a privilege to know the bard's daughter, Morag Cumming. She provided invaluable information and photographs and has a special gift for bringing out the wit in her father's songs.

Dr. Anya Gunderloch discovered the manuscript copy of *Aeòlus* in a box in the Celtic Department in Glasgow University where it had slumbered undisturbed since 1968.

The late Peter Bowie, Howbeg, was a very useful source of local information.

Murdo Macleod of Lewis and Inverness cast his expert eye over the manuscript at an early stage and Ishabel T. MacDonald supervised the recording of the verse.

Dr. Margaret Bennett and Dr. Gonzalo J. Mazzei did much to bolster my flagging morale when the project seemed in danger of foundering.

Finally, my thanks to Sandy Stanage for his imaginative original musical interpretation. Sandy was so captivated by the rhythms and sound of Macintyre's verse that he spent many hours more on the project than duty alone required.

Bill Innes 2008

Introduction

"It is as though one of the 18th century poets had been alive in our midst in the 20th century. Here we find the same teeming vocabulary, the same fluency in using Gaelic, the same mastery of metre. Yet the poetry is undeniably of our time in its subject matter and its attitudes ..."

Professor Derick Thomson

Donald Macintyre, *Dòmhnall Ruadh Mac an t-Saoir*, is best remembered today for comic songs such as *Sporan Dhòmhnaill, Bùth Dhòmhnaill 'ic Leòid* and *Oran na Cloiche* which were once the staple fare of the ceilidh. They linger on in famous recordings by Captain Donald Joseph Mackinnon (*An Eòsag*). But anyone who has read his collected poetry (*Sporan Dhòmhnaill*, Scottish Gaelic Texts Society 1968) will know that such songs were but the superficial gloss on the brilliance of his talent.

His masterwork, *Aeòlus agus am Balg*, won him the bardic crown of *An Comunn Gàidhealach* at the 1938 National Mod in Glasgow. One of the judges hailed it then as "the Gaelic poem of the century ..." In this new century it must still be regarded as one of the finest examples of the art and power of the traditional bard. As with all his poetry, the full effect can only be realised if it is read aloud.

Dòmhnall Ruadh was born in 1889 in Snishival, South Uist at a time when the life of a crofter was poverty-stricken and arduous. With all its best arable machair land allocated to tacksmen, Snishival struggled to support more than twenty families on poor moorland. It was, however, a rich storehouse of Gaelic oral tradition. The ruins of Donald's birthplace can still be seen (2008) next to a large house which dominates the skyline. In its heyday as a ceilidh house his father's humble thatched cottage was such a forum for debate, storytelling, music and poetry that it was known locally as *An Colaiste* (The College)!

Although his father Angus, *Aonghas Ruadh*, was a quiet and unassuming man, his mother Kate, *Ceit Ruadh*, had a much more lively personality with a rich fund of songs, stories and prayers. A daughter of Angus MacLean, *Am Pìobaire Bàn*, she was also proficient at *canntaireachd* — the system of oral transmission of pipe music. The piper Rona Lightfoot tells the story that, as a little girl of four, Kate returned from the machair singing in *canntaireachd* a tune that no one recognised. When asked where she had heard it, she replied, "From the fairies!" — a story she maintained till her dying day. Rona calls the tune *Ceit Ruadh's Reel*. There was a belief amongst traditional bards that their talent passed down through the maternal line, so it seems reasonable to agree with the editor of *Sporan Dhòmhnaill*, Somerled Macmillan, that Donald inherited most of his gifts from her.

Despite obvious intelligence, Donald had to leave school at fourteen. His leaving certificate testifies to the wide range of subjects studied at the little two-roomed Howmore school — with the conspicuous exception of Gaelic. (As in some other Uist schools of the time, head teacher Winifred Bird was English.) Apparently a visiting school inspector said of him, "That little red-haired boy could be Chancellor of the Exchequer!" He did win at least one prize — a book of Burns' poetry. This was to prove a major influence, as his superb paraphrase of *Tam o' Shanter* bears witness.[1]

When the tacks of Milton and Bornish were broken up at the beginning of the 20th century, the family moved to a new home in Kildonan. This house later became the home of another famous Uist bard, Donald Allan MacDonald — who married Catherine, a daughter of Donald's eldest sister Flora. The belief that the bardic gift was transmitted through the maternal line gained further credence when another sister, Margaret, married the renowned *seanchaidh* (storyteller) Duncan MacDonald. Their son, Donald John MacDonald, *Dòmhnall Iain Dhonnchaidh*, became yet another great poet.[2]

While *Dòmhnall Ruadh* had no singing voice, he became

---

[1] *Sporan Dhòmhnaill* p.315

[2] See *Chì Mi, The Poetry of Donald John MacDonald* (Birlinn 2001)

a fine piper and dancer. In the 1914-18 war he served in the Cameron Highlanders as Locheil's regimental piper. After the war, jobs were hard to come by. The graphic description of the storm at sea in *Aeòlus* probably owes much to the time he spent as a fisherman, but he had to leave Uist to earn a living and eventually found a trade as a bricklayer in Paisley.

In 1930 he married Mary Maclellan. Despite the many humorous but affectionate grumbles about his wife in his songs, they were by all accounts a devoted couple. They had four children and his eldest daughter, Morag Cumming, became an excellent interpreter of her father's songs.

Like many other intelligent islanders, Donald made up for his lack of formal education by wide reading and lively discussion. The late Cathal Campbell said that when he was studying Moral Philosophy at Glasgow University it was Donald who clarified matters for him over an evening pint in the pub!

However, *Aoir an Luchd-Riaghlaidh*[3] shows how much it must have hurt the bard that his lack of formal qualifications prevented his work being taken seriously by the academic establishment.

> Ged nach deach mi fo òrdugh
> A' giùlan còta na clèire,
> 'S ged nach robh mi nam sgoilear
> Bho Ard-thaigh-oilein Dhun Eideann,
> Chumainn fosgailte m' inntinn,
> Dhèanainn sgrìobhadh is leughadh,
> Bhruidhninn Beurl' agus Gàidhlig —
> Ach dh'fhanainn sàmhach is dh'èistinn
> A cheart cho math!

> Although I was not ordained
> Wearing a clerical coat
> And though I was not a scholar
> Of Edinburgh University,

---

3 *Sporan Dhòmhnaill* p.266

I would keep an open mind,
I could read and write,
I could speak English and Gaelic —
But I could stay silent and listen
        Just as well!

His later poems reflect an increasing awareness of mortality as
he struggled with failing health. After a bad fall, he died on 7th
January 1964 and is buried in Hawkhead Cemetery, Paisley. The
grave was marked by a splendid new stone in 2001.

A very moving and powerful elegy, *Do Dhòmhnall
Ruadh Mac an t-Saoir*,[4] was composed by his nephew Donald
John MacDonald. A verse from it was used on the simple cairn
at the side of the main A865 road in Snishival by which both
men are now jointly commemorated.

> *Dh'fhàg thu dìleab tha luachmhor*
> *Mar bheath' a dh'inntinn an t-sluaigh tha dhed nàisean,*
> *Beairteas litreachais phrìseil*
> *'S e gu gibhteil leat sgrìobht' ann am bàrdachd:*
> *Chuir do sheirbheis 's gach cuspair dhith*
> *Fuil bu deirg' ann an cuislean na Gàidhlig*
> *'S bidh air mhaireann do bhriathran*
> *Ged bhios do cholainn a' crìonadh am Pàislig.*

> You left a precious legacy
> To nourish the spirit of your people,
> A priceless treasure of literature,
> Giftedly written in verse:
> Your work in every part of it
> Put reddest blood in the veins of Gaelic
> And your words will survive
> Though your body crumbles in Paisley.

---

4 *Chì Mi* (Birlinn 2001) p.218

The Poetry

The loss of old values and the abandonment of Gaelic with increasing material prosperity were recurrent themes in Macintyre's work.

Tha tìr nam beanntan air fàs cho Gallda
Chan fhaodar seann rud a thoirt à cùil
'S a' chànan aosda bha 'm bial nan daoine
Ga leigeadh aog ann le cion an diù:
Nach mòr an tàmailt ma chanas càch e
Gun tug sinn àite do chànain ùr
'S mo chuimhne fhèin ann nach cluinnt' de Bheurl' ann
Air latha fèilleadh na chaisgeadh cù!
Oran air Cor na Gàidhlig

The land of bens has grown so Lowland,
Old things must be hidden away
And the ancient speech of the people
Allowed to die there through lack of esteem:
How great the shame if others can say
That we gave a place to another tongue
When I can't remember hearing on a feast-day
As much English as would curb a dog!

In the latter half of the 20th century Gaelic poetry moved away from traditional bardic verse (recited or sung) towards a more literary style. As Donald's nephew, Donald John MacDonald, said: "Once we made songs to be sung; now we write poetry to be read." In the new orthodoxy contemporary traditional verse was deemed parochial and restrictive of subject matter; its composers dismissed as mere *bàird-baile* (village poets).

The rise of the new poetry coincided with the disappearance of the ceilidh house forum. This, together with a general decline in the richness of the spoken language, deprived bards of their natural audience. In despair at lack of recognition, Donald was about to put all his poetry on the fire when his daughter Morag caught him only just in time. Sadly, he was never to see his collected works in print — for *Sporan Dhòmhnaill* was not published till four years after his death.

In 1999, however, Ronald Black had this to say in the introduction to *An Tuil*, his mammoth collection of 20th century Gaelic verse;

> ... the posthumous publication in 1968 of *Sporan Dhòmhnaill*, the collected works of Donald Macintyre, had provided the first real opportunity to assess the case for 20th century traditional poetry on its merits; to me at least, this book arrived like a bombshell, blowing up all the old certainties about the superiority of the 'new' verse that I had imbibed since arriving at university in 1964.

Songs like *Oran na Cloiche*[5] demonstrate a passionate love of country and consequent Scottish nationalism. He must have had more than an armchair interest in politics; his daughter Morag relates that two of the young students who removed the Stone of Scone from Westminster Abbey visited her father on their return from England. Although his political inclination was to the left, Donald found that perfectly compatible with respect for the Royal Family. He wrote two elegies on the death of King George VI. The first, commissioned by the BBC, is conventional but the other, *Marbhrann eile don Rìgh*,[6] is in a more personal style and clearly composed from the heart. He celebrated the crowning of the young Queen in another two songs.

However, *Aoir an Luchd-Riaghlaidh* mentioned above shows a healthy contempt for the pretensions of the rich and of the politicians who had failed his generation between the wars. Having worked hard all his life, he was equally cynical about Union barons who used their members to further personal quests for power. This was made clear in *Then* and *Now* – an unpublished English poem of over 350 lines which was a passionate cry for justice for the ordinary working man.

---

[5] SD p. 147

[7] SD p. 256

Anon the Union delegate comes round ...
... A keen-eyed sentinel on watch and ward
To see that no-one works without a card
With all its weekly contributions paid —
A rule that must be never disobeyed.

These haughty chieftains of the TUC
Collect their cash from chaps like you and me,
For otherwise they'd have to pay their bus,
To earn their bread and butter just like us;
To sit at table with the common mass
Instead of dining with the upper class.

He notes with glee the sulky, sullen looks
Of certain men receiving certain books
And to the boss he mutters, "That's the stuff —
Get rid of every bold and brass-faced tough;
We won't have independents on a job —
We are the masters of the toiling mob;
We brook no rebels that defy our will —
An empty paunch will bring the hounds to heel."

Like many other bards, Donald was influenced through the oral
tradition by a wide range of the great names of Gaelic culture
while he educated himself in English literature through reading.
That school prize book of Burns had triggered his admiration
for Scotland's national poet. He did a fine translation of *The Twa
Dugs*[7] but his version of *Tam o' Shanter*[8] is a masterly paraphrase
which converted the Scots to melodious, idiomatic Gaelic. His
Còmhradh eadar an t-Seann Tè 's an Tè Ur[9] is a partial paraphrase
of *The Brigs of Ayr* (wrongly identified in *Sporan Dhòmhnaill* as
a slanging match between two human protagonists). He also
set some of his songs to Burns' tunes — notably *Mo Mhaighdean
Og*,[10] a lovely tribute to his daughter Catherine set to *O' a' the*

---

[7] SD p. 327
[8] SD p. 315
[9] SD p. 98
[10] SD p.100

Airts the Wind Can Blaw.

However, his claim to a place in the premier division of traditional Gaelic bards rests with the two great epics *MacPhàil is MacThòmais*[11] and *Aeòlus agus am Balg*.[12]

The former runs to over 850 lines and is modelled on Duncan Bàn Macintyre's *Moladh Beinn Dòbhrain*. Starting with a bitingly witty attack on two men in Locheynort who had neglected croft and home through idleness, it broadens into successive hymns of praise for all the traditional work they should have done. It includes one of the most lyrical and rhythmic descriptions of peat-cutting ever composed!

Aeòlus

In the preparation of this edition, I was fortunate to have access to the original ms which had just been rediscovered in the archives of Glasgow University. As Donald had had to teach himself to read and write Gaelic, his spelling was erratic and punctuation and capital letters were usually conspicuous by their absence. While the opportunity has been taken to correct a few errors of transcription which occurred in *Sporan Dhòmhnaill*, the manuscript did confirm that assonance occasionally took priority over strict rules of grammar and sound. Accents were present only to indicate that a vowel sound should be lengthened in the interests of assonance.

Aeòlus is an undoubted masterpiece. Its 716 lines are really four different poems on the central theme of a great storm which caused widespread destruction in Uist in 1921. In particular, it blew away the thatched roof of a house near to the bard's birthplace. Although by then the family had moved to Kildonan, this may have influenced the original inspiration.

There is an even longer poem on a similar subject by Donald Sinclair of Barra. *Latha nan Seachd Sìon* was published serially in *Guth na Bliadhna* in 1915-16. Like *Aeòlus*, it tells of the effects of a great storm on land and sea and how the crisis is resolved through the power of prayer. Macintyre would

---

[11] SD p. 102

[12] SD p. 61

undoubtedly have been familiar with it — if only through his great friend and interpreter of his songs, Captain DJ Mackinnon.

His stroke of genius was to see the storm as an unholy conspiracy between *Æolus* (the Greek god of the winds), *Neptune* (the Roman god of the sea) and *Thor* (the Norse god of the thunder) to destroy Scotland. Given the time of its composition in 1938, the poem is also an allegory of that other unholy alliance of Hitler, Mussolini and Hirohito with the objective of world domination.

The British are accustomed to think of World War II as starting in 1939, but by 1938 Hitler had already taken over Austria and Czechoslovakia, Japan had invaded China and Mussolini was attempting to further his own ambitions in Africa. Certainly the bluster of the pagan gods includes an apocalyptic vision of the Armageddon to come which would sit more easily in the mouths of fascist dictators.

Æolus to Neptune:

> *"Bailtean mòra dol nam fàsach*
> *Sealladh as àille lem shùil;*
> *Làn de chuirp 's gun duin' air fhàgail*
> *A their àite dhaibh san ùir.*
>
> *"Garachd an fhithich, gloc na farspaig*
> *Is iad a' sracadh ann an cairbh,*
> *Air an tachdadh leis a' ghionach,*
> *Agus milleanan dhiubh marbh."*

> > "Great cities turned to wasteland —
> > A sight my eyes love to see;
> > Full of bodies, with no one left
> > To lay them in the ground.
> >
> > "Croak of raven, black-back's cry
> > As they tear at corpses,
> > Choking with gluttony
> > As millions lie dead."

Clearly this has little to do with a mere storm in Uist.
Later, Neptune to Æolus:

> *"Cuim' a dh'fhanainn air mo chrìochan?*
> *Cuim' nach leudaichinn mo ghart?*
> *Cuim' nach buannaichinn an saoghal*
> *Is gun tèid daonnan neart thar cheart?"*

> "Why stay within my bounds?
> Why not widen my estate?
> Why not take over the world,
> When might will always conquer right?"

In bringing these mythical gods terrifyingly alive Donald uses ancient traditional metres with a facility which not many of the old masters achieved. The poem builds in a crescendo of wonderfully musical and idiomatic Gaelic, then changes down a gear before climbing again to one climax after another as he describes the impact of the storm on Uist crofter and Scandinavian sailing ship alike.

Padraig Mòr, who features in the second section, is based on a real person — Patrick MacDonald, *Pàdraig mac Dhòmhnaill 'ic Fhearghais 'ic Phàdraig*, who lived close to the main road at Milton. The verses on his preparations for the storm may have been inspired by the effect of the storm on the thatched house of Donald's ex-neighbour in Snishival mentioned above.

In the section on the Norse ship the poet's love of the sea tempts him into a digression on historical and technical details which slows dramatic development, but the pace soon builds again. When the metre changes to twelve line verses, there is a temporary shift into first person narration as he imagines himself part of the action. In the end all is drawn to a satisfying conclusion when the ancient pagan gods are forced to concede that they must yield before a greater Christian God.

As in all of Donald's work, the words flow in a rich, rhythmic river of sound which enhances the meaning so powerfully that the poem can only be appreciated fully when read aloud. It is sad if a decline in the quality of spoken Gaelic has made his work less accessible to a modern audience. The importance of appreciating the sound of such poetry is one of the greatest incentives for keeping Gaelic alive as a living, breathing, spoken language of the people.

It is also the reason that it was considered essential to include a CD with this present volume. It is hoped that this recording will help the reader to understand why that adjudicator in 1938 hailed *Aeòlus agus am Balg* as the Gaelic poem of the century. It is a wonderful example of the power of a great traditional bard, giving the lie to those who would argue that the conventions of traditional poetry are too restrictive to cope with modern concepts. As with any truly great work of art, it is accessible on more than one level.

The Metres

The rules of rhyme and metre in Gaelic traditional verse are so complex that some modern poets are only too happy to dismiss them as restrictive and old-fashioned. The more honest will admit that few today have the richness of vocabulary necessary to comply with the rules of rhyme without undue repetition.

The bards believed their talent to be inborn and independent of education. Donald Allan MacDonald of South Uist said:

> *"Chan eil do dh'fhoghlam air an t-saoghal a dhèanadh duine na bhàrd..."* [There is not enough education in the world to make a man a bard...][13]

Gaelic rhyme is more correctly described as assonance, as it concerns vowel sounds only. Onomatopoeia, whereby the sound of the words reinforces the sense, is a vital part of the art. Another important characteristic is the use of concrete imagery drawn from nature rather than the symbolism of the modern writer. The remarkable feats of memory of the seanchaidhs and

---

13 The Songs of Donald Allan Macdonald (Federation of Southern Isles Historical Socs. 1999) p.30

bards were in some part due to their ability to visualise their works as a stream of mental pictures – thereby making use of both halves of the brain.

The first three cantos of *Aeòlus*, dealing with the conspiracy of the pagan gods, *Pàdraig Mòr's* preparations for the storm and the sailing of the Norse tall ship, are all in the same centuries-old classical stressed metre – *dàn dìreach*. The verses are quatrains consisting of two rhyming couplets. Each couplet consists of two lines of eight syllables and features internal rhyme — *aicill* — between the last syllables of the first line and syllables in the middle of the second line. This common feature of traditional poetry was an invaluable aid to memory in poems as long as this one.

Alliteration or *uaim* (consecutive words starting with the same sound) was one of the standard devices which helped to embellish the all-important sound of the verse. The particular case where the consecutive words are at the end of a line is known as *fior-uaim*. Notice that short unstressed words in between an alliterative pair do not count.

Consider this fine example from Neptune's exhortation to Æolus:

> Sèid gun aiteal, sèid gun abhsadh,
> Seid le bladadh a ni cnead;
> Sèid gu gnuadha, gruamach, gailbheach,
> Fuaraidh, fearghasach le fead.

The couplets rhyme *cnead* with *fead*, but within each there is *aicill* which may not be so obvious on the printed page. The recording makes clear that *abhsadh* rhymes with *bladadh* and *gailbheach* (pronounced as three syllables) with *fearghasach*. The alliteration in the second couplet is masterly with repeated *g* and *f* consonants reinforced by repeated *ua* diphthongs. The whole verse is a wonderful evocation of the howl of the gale and no translation could do it justice.

The last section of the poem consists of fifteen twelve-line verses with four triplets in each verse. This stressed metre was used by such 17th century bards as *Iain Lom* MacDonald, e.g. *Iorram do Bhàta MhicDhòmhnaill*, a rowing song for Sir James

MacDonald's Galley, which is sung by Rev. William Matheson on the School of Scottish Studies CD *Gaelic Bards and Minstrels*. Each triplet can be considered as three rhyming lines of seven syllables with a tag line of three syllables.

> Ged a *bheagadh a h-aodach*
> Cha do *sheas i ach slaodach*
> 'S cha do *leasaich air saothair* / nan Tuathach

In this particular example there is assonance between the last five syllables of the lines of the triplet. Even a bard of Donald's virtuosity could not maintain that discipline consistently, but his vocabulary is so rich that we are rarely conscious of the rules which govern his choice of words. Occasionally he claims poetic licence to allow assonance priority over strict rules of grammar. However, each of the sixty tag lines throughout the fifteen verses rhymes the *ua* diphthong — with hardly any duplication!

The importance of sound to traditional poetry has meant that it has not always been possible to follow strictly the rules of the Gaelic Orthographic Conventions which became de rigueur for educational publications long after the poet had died. Where the bard's Uist sound did not fit the rules, his usage has been given priority. It is perfectly proper to establish conventions for new writing, but these should not be allowed to have a retrospective influence on the sound of traditional poetry — whether that be in the Scots of Burns or the Gaelic of Donald Macintyre.

The bard uses *do* for *de* and also the *ia* dipthong in words like *eun* and *beul* where assonance requires the Uist sound. The common abbreviation for *agus* varies between *is* and *'s*. (In the former case, a vestigial vowel sound can be suggested without affecting the metre.) These usages have been retained

Readers will have their own views on that verdict of the 1938 adjudicator's that this was the Gaelic poem of the 20th century. However, as an epic traditional ballad dealing with 20th century events in allegorical form, *Aeòlus* can more confidently claim to be unique in the Gaelic corpus.

Bill Innes 2008

Donald Macintyre's birthplace (*An Colaiste*) in the 1950s. At left is the ruin of the house which lost its thatch in the 1921 storm.

Donald (in his WWI Cameron Highlanders uniform) with his father Angus.

His mother Kate, *Ceit Ruadh,* was an important tradition bearer and early influence.

Top Left: Donald & Mary in Uist 1955. Despite the many pretend grumbles in his songs, they were a devoted couple.

Top Right: Donald with his son Angus after a good day of (illicit) angling.

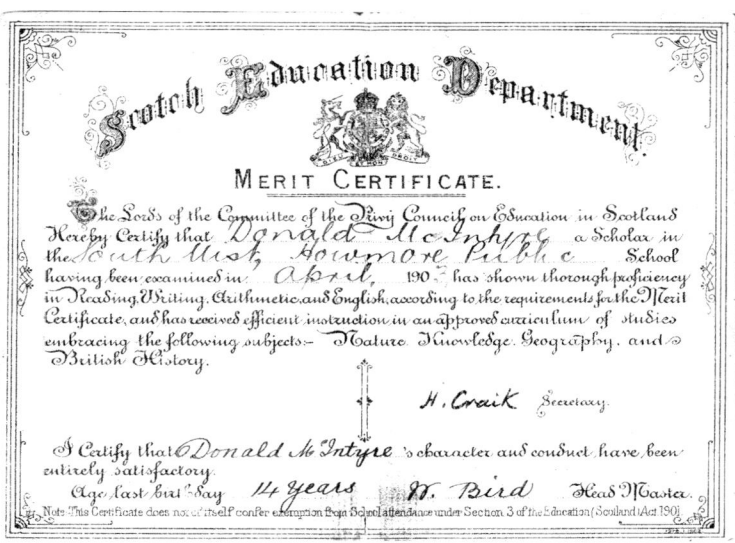

His leaving certificate from Howmore School. Everything but Gaelic!

71 Broomlands Street
Paisley
Renfrewshire
                29 Aug 1957

My Dear Eosag
        Just a wee note to let you
know how sorry I was not to get home to visit
This year I missed it although I enjoyed my
holiday in Kingussie very much a lovely
place it is but no gaelic, the only gaelic I got
apart from Morag and Donhall Ban was
two old men from roy bridge both of them
blind who were in the sanatorium I had
plenty of talk with them and they knew
the people I used to know when I was
working with Balfour Beattie at roy bridge
I heard your voice over the wireless the
other night singing the rockets and you
made a good job of it. I must thank
you very much for the money yo sent
me my wife never gave it to me nor let
me know till I was actually in the train
going to Kingussie you will understand why
yourself but you should not send any
more to me you deserve it all yourself
well now you were telling me the last
time I saw you the priest was fond of my
song of the Rabbit well I am enclosing it
rearranged and far bigger than it was before
I took nothing out of it but added a lot of
verses that you havent heard before I am
also sending my translation of Dork Lochnagar
and if you practice it and sing it Its a
beautiful tune and I made a good job of the
translation I'll maybe hear you on the BB.C.
singing it yet. I must tell you I got a
letter from Sydney australia from somebody
who is a proffessor of scottish history and a
bachelor of arts he wanted my translation
of Burns's tam-o-shanter how he heard
about me I dont know but I sent him a
copy anyway so I must close now we are
all in our usual health hoping you and
yours are the same, I remain your
sincere friend
                Donald Mac Intyre

A letter to his friend and well-known interpreter of his songs, Captain Donald Joseph Mackinnon, *An Eòsag*. The songs referred to, including *Na Rocaidean, Gearain a' Choineinich, Loch nan Geàrr* and *Tòmas Seanntair*, can all be found in *Sporan Dhòmhnaill*.

Neptune.. a.g. eirigh

dh eirich Neptune suas le mhorgha
as e ga chonnalachadh an àirde
mar lann bhiodh os cionn a ghruailadh
aig curaidh a ruagadh namhaid

b aogmuidh an sealladh fo bhuaras,
righ nan stuadh bu ghruamach colg
momhadas, ardan, as uamhar,
a dearrsadh na ghruaidhean gorm

bu naimhdail a mhuing gheal-chopach
air druim cnocach a chuain mhòir
sa h uile calg inute g eighach
gun be chreidsan sicumhachdii còir ✓

ge be shealladh air na speuran
bha e leirsinnach ni fhaicean
aig an t-ùil dha m b eol a leughadh
gun ro fearg na beistadh laiste

A page from the manuscript discovered in Glasgow University Celtic Department. Donald had taught himself to read and write Gaelic, so spelling and punctuation could be erratic, accents were rarely included (unless to indicate unusual stresses – see Notes) and proper names rarely had capital letters.

Left: Donald in Uist in 1955

Below: Son Angus, Donald, Mary and daughter Catherine.

His daughters— Catherine, Morag and Ann

© Margaret Walker

© Bill Innes

Top Left: Cpt. Donald J. Mackinnon, *An Eòsag*, who popularised many of Donald's songs.

Top Right: The headstone in Hawkhead cemetery.

© Bill Innes

The joint memorial to Donald John MacDonald and Donald Macintyre unveiled by their daughters, Margaret Campbell and Morag Cumming, in 1996.

Earrann I

TR -2

Ordugh Aeòluis don Bhalg

Labhair Aeòlus, "Sèid, mo bhalg,   **1**
Pronn an calg is frois an gràn,
Rùisg na taighean, spìon am fraoch,
Leag na craobhan sìos ri làr.

"Riab is siab is brist is sgealb,
Ardaich m' ainm-sa measg nan dùl,
Nochd do dh'innleachdan chlann-daoine
Meud am faoineis nam dhà shùil.

"Sèid gu daingeann, sèid gu cruaidh,
Sèid gun iochd, gun truas, gun chàs,   **10**
Sèid le uile chlì do ghuailleadh,
Sgrìob do sguaibeadh — faiceam à!

"Gainne is gort is gaoiribh guil,
Sgrios is tuil is call is àr;
Faiceam geilt an gnùis an t-sluaigh,
'S ait leam gruaidhean fhaicinn bàn.

Movement I

TR-2

Æolus gives Orders to his Bellows

1   Thus spake Æolus, "Blow, my bellows,
Crush the corn and thresh the grain,
Strip the houses, tear the heather,
Fell the trees unto the ground.

"Rend and sweep, smash and splinter,
Amongst the elements raise my fame,
Prove to the puny works of man
How slight they stand before my eyes.

"Blow full force, blow your hardest,
10   Without compassion, mercy, fear,
Blow with all your strength of arm,
Your swathe of sweeping — show it me!

"Famine, want and cries of pain,
Destruction, flood, loss and strife;
Show me people struck with fear —
I laugh to see their faces white.

"Faiceam ainmhidhean a' crùbadh
Anns gach toll is cùil is càrn,
Sireadh iasg an t-aigeal gorm
Is mise, dia na stoirm, ga ràdh!   **20**

"O 's e cumhachd còir is ceart,
Feuch mo neart air muir is tìr,
Sir 's na seachainn sean na òg
Is thar gach seòrsa tog mo chìs.

"'S coingeis leanabh na fear liath,
'S coingeis feòil na iasg leam ann;
'S coingeis duine, brùid no ian;
Sgaoil mo lìon o cheann gu ceann.

"Tarraing sgrìob an lùib nam beò,
Brist nan dòchas ioma neach   **30**
Is nochd do chumhachd mhòr, a bhuilg,
Ann ad luirg biodh sgeul nan creach.

"Let me see animals cower
In every nook and hole and cairn,
Let fish seek the ocean floor —
So I, the god of storms, declare!

"As power is the might and right,
Test my strength on land and sea;
Seek and spare not young or old —
Exact my dues from every kind.

"I care not whether babe or sage,
I care not whether flesh or fish;
Whether man or beast or bird,
Spread my net from end to end.

"Cut a swathe through the living,
Destroy the hopes of many a one;
Show your mighty strength, my bellows,
Leave tales of ruin in your wake."

20

30

TR-3

Aeòlus a' Bòilich

"Tha mo chuireadh farsaing, fial,
Fad' is cian feadh thriath is dhùl:
Iad a chruinneachadh o gach taobh
Is gheibh iad saor mo chuirm-chiùil.

"Teachdaire nan casan sgiathach
A bhith triall gan toirt gu teachd,
Eadar far an deàrrs a' ghrian
Is far nach fhacas riamh ach sneachd.   **40**

"A h-uile h-aon fhear shìos no shuas
Air an d' fhuaradh lideadh sgeòil
A thàinig o chluais gu cluais
Am measg nan sluagh le aithris beòil,

"A chaidh air cloich no clàr a sgrìobhadh,
No chuir filidhean an ruinn
Gan aiseag on tìm a bha
A-nuas o phàrantan gu cloinn.

Æolus Blustering

"My invitation is open, broad
To gods and elements, far and wide;
Let them come from every side
And they shall have my music free.

"Let the messenger of winged feet [1]
Be on his way to bring them here,
From between where sun shines bright
To where only snow was ever seen.

"Every each one, here and there
Ever mentioned in a tale
Handed on from ear to ear
Amongst the folk by word of mouth,

"Or ever writ on stone or page,
Or that poets set in verse,
Passed on from olden times,
Down from parent on to child.

40

7

"Creideamh na h-aimsir a thriall
Do chuan na sìorraidheachd nach trèig   **50**
Am fad bhios an ainmeannan beò,
Cho fad 's 'ios cuimhn' air Tròidh is Grèig,

"Air an luaidh an cainnt a' bhàird —
Homer as àirde ann an cliù:
Cruinnicheadh iad 's gum faigh iad ceòl
Nach d' fhuair an Fhèinn mu Chòrn nam Fiùdh'.

"Leigidh mi mo ghaoth thar lomhainn
As a tollaibh domhainn duaichnidh;
Is cluinnidh linn gun teachd oirr' aisneis
Mun tig i air n-ais gu h-uaimhidh."   **60**

"Beliefs of ages long gone
50   To the eternal, everlasting sea:
So long will their names live on
As Troy and Greece are kept in mind,

"Praised in the words of the bard —
Homer of highest renown;[2]
Let them gather to hear more music
Than heard the Feinn from Fingal's horn.[3]

"I'll let my tempest off its leash,
Out from its deep, dark den;
Generations unborn will hear the tale
60   Before it returns to its cave."

9

TR-4

Aeòlus ri Thòr

"Siud mo ghlaodh thugad, a Thòir,
Gus an t-òrd a dhol na dheann
Is teine dealain lasrach, geur
Bhith sracadh brat nan speur gum bonn."

"On as ionmhainn leat an stoirm
Cluinneam dorraraich buillean t' ùird, [4]
A' cur dhaoin' air chrith le fhuaim
'S a' cur luasgan air gach brùid.

"Tilg do bheithrichean a-nuas,
Rùisg is ruamhair uchd nam beann;   70
Cnuic is garbhlaichean nan stùc
A' falbh nan sprùilleach sìos le gleann."

TR-4

Æolus to Thor

"Thus my cry to you, O Thor —
Let the hammer blows fall thick
And fire of lightning, piercing, bright,
Shall rend the curtained skies apart.

"As you love the storm so much,
Let me hear your hammer ring,
Making men shiver at its sound
And every beast to quake with fear.

"Hurl your thunderbolts down,
Denude and blast the mountain slopes,
Hills and rocks of the stacks
Tumbling piecemeal down the glen."

70

Aeòlus ri Neptune

"Dùisg, a Neptune, às do shuain,
Piopraich suas an cuan gu strì;
Faiceam colg air cìrein stuadh
Gu còmhrag chruaidh a chur ri tìr.

"Leum air Alb' o cheann gu ceann,
Crath a beanntannan gum bonn;
Eireadh fairge ghorm rin gnùis
Is bidh neart mo bhuilg ri cùl nan tonn.   **80**

"Fùidse dha cloich-ghràine ghlais
'S tric a chais mi oirr' on iar;
Ach a dh'aindeoin neart mo bhuilg,
Cha deach tulg na stèidhe riamh.

"Ge-ta, chan eil ormsa sgàth,
'S binn leam gàir nan còmhrag gharg,
'S ait leam gleac ri gaisgeach treun,
Fear nach gèill dhomh fhèin 's dham bhalg."

Æolus to Neptune

"Awake, O Neptune, from your sleep
Incite the ocean up to strife,
Let me see the breakers' fury
Wage bitter war upon the land.

"Leap on Scotland from end to end
Shake her mountains to their roots;
Green seas shall rise against them,
My bellows' force behind the waves.

80

"Challenge its grey granite stone
Which oft I swooped on from the west —
But for all my bellows' power,
Its foundation never rocked.

"But that does not worry me,
For whom fierce battles' roar is sweet;
I prefer to fight a warrior bold
Who resists my bellows' might and me."

13

TR-5

Neptune ag Eirigh

Dh'èirich Neptune suas le mhòrghath
Is e ga chonalachadh an-àirde   90
Mar lann bhiodh os cionn a ghuailleadh
Aig curaidh a' ruagadh nàmhaid.

B' aognaidh an sealladh fo bhuaireas
Rìgh nan stuadh bu ghruamach colg —
Nàmhadas, àrdan is uabhar
A' deàrrsadh na ghruaidhean gorm.

Bu nàimhdeil a mhuing gheal-chopach
Air druim cnocach a' chuain mhòir,
'S a h-uile calg innt' ag èigheach
Gum b' e chreud-san, " 'S cumhachd còir".   100

Ge b' e shealladh air na speuran,
Bha e lèirsinneach ri fhaicinn,
Aig an t-sùil dham b' eòl a leughadh,
Gun robh fearg na bèisteadh laiste.

Neptune Arising

Up rose Neptune brandishing
90   His trident high aloft,
Like the spear of a warrior raised
To drive his enemies out.

Awesome was the raging sight —
King of the waves in sullen fury;
Fierce, haughty aggression
Glaring from his sea-green cheeks.

Angry was his white foaming mane
On the heaving surface of the sea,
With every bristle there proclaiming
100   That his creed was, "Might is right".

Whoever looked to the skies,
It was obvious to see,
For the eye with skill to read,
That the brute's anger was aflame.

Sheall e mun cuairt air a rìoghachd,
Dh'fhosgail a chuinneanan farsaing
'S e deas gu glacadh na chrùidhean
Aon a thigeadh air oighreachd tarsainn.

Thilg e bàta mòr na smùideadh
Bun-os-cionn leis a làimh làidir —   **110**
I fhèin 's na bh' innte gan giùlan,
Thug e 'n grunnd mar àite-tàimh dhi.

Sloc a h-uaghach air a dhùnadh,
Gun fear innse-sgiùil air fhàgail,
"Sin dhut leab' tha farsaing, sùmhail,
Far am faod na giùdhrain fàs ort."

Nuair a laigh i air an aigeal,
Ghearr e stailleag is rinn e gàire,
Choc e smigid is shìn e sgòrnan
A' cur bòst à neart a ghàirdein.   **120**

He glared around his kingdom
His nostrils flaring wide,
Ready to grasp in his clutches
Any who dared to cross his realm.

He tossed the great steamship
110 Upside down with his mighty arm,
Giving her and all on board
The bottom for a resting-place.

The pit of her grave having closed
With no one left to tell the tale,
"There's a broad and peaceful bed
Where barnacles can cover you."

When she rested in the deep,
He snapped his fingers, laughed aloud,
Cocked his chin and stretched his throat
120 Boasting of his strength of arm.

Neptune a' Bòilich

Dh'èibh e, "'S mise rìgh nan tonn;
'S mis' an sonn a dhearbh mo ghnìomh;
'S mise riaghladair nan stuadh
A deas 's a tuath 's an ear 's an iar.

"'S mise fear an eallaich mhòir,
'S mi tha beòthail air mo bhuinn;
Cha toir aois air falbh mo threòir;
Tha mi òg o linn gu linn.

"Tha mo bheartas maireann buan,
Cus nas luachmhoire na 'n t-òr   **130**
Is e cho pailt 's nach fhairichinn bhuam
Na chaidh riamh a bhuain dhem stòr.

"Glaiste, ceangailte fom dheigheann
'S lionmhor seud is àille snuadh
Nach leig innleachd dhaoine ris
Fhad 's bhios mise os cionn a' chuain.

"'S mis' an gaisgeach nach eil faoin,
'S ann nam ghaoirdean a tha 'n tàth;
Seall air Carraig Leum MhicNeacail —
Mis' a shrac i mach o chàch.   **140**

Neptune Boasting

He cried, "I am the king of waves,
The warrior who proved his deeds;
I am ruler of the seas,
North and south, west and east.

"I am he of the mighty burden,
I am so lively on my toes,
Old age will not sap my strength;
Through the centuries I stay young.

"My treasure is everlasting,
130   Much more precious than gold,
So ample that I would not miss
All ever taken from my store.

"Locked and bound with my chains, [5]
Many are the loveliest gems
That all man's skill will not reveal
So long as I rule upon the seas.

"I am no weakling warrior,
It is my arm that has the strength;
See the Rock of Nicholson's Leap —[6]
140   It was I who ripped it from the rest.

"Mis' a chladhaich Uamha 'n Sgòthaidh
A-steach an sgòrnan na clach-ghràin,
Mis' a dh'iomain Mol nan Dòrnag,
'S mi rinn còmhnard an Traigh Bhàn.

"Tha clann-daoine rium a' sabaid
On chaidh maid' a chur air snàmh,
Eadar sin 's am bàta cruadhach
Dùbailte mun cuairt a' mhàis.

"Ach a dh'aindheoin an cuid innleachd
Bidh mo chìs orra gu bràth   **150**
Is fhad 's a bhios mo dhruim gan giùlan
Togaidh mise dhiùbh mo mhàl.

"'S mis' an steud nach fuiling srian,
Nach gabh ciallachadh no stad;
Cò chuir deigheann air mo shàil
O laigh an Airc air Ararat?

"'S mis' tha daonnan deas gu còmhstri —
Suas sinn, Aeòluis, glòir dhar n-ainm;
Mis' is tusa 'n taic a chèile,
Hò rò èile, sèid am balg!"   **160**

"It was I who dug the Sgothaidh Cave [7]
Into the throat of the granite rock;
I created the Pebble Beach,
I made level the White Strand.[8]

"Mankind have always challenged me
Since the first stick was set afloat,
Between then and the steel ship
With the plated double hull.

"But for all their inventions
150   I will forever take my toll;
So long as men ride my back
I will raise from them my dues.

"I am the steed that brooks no rein,
That cannot be tamed or curbed;
Who has ever chained my heels [9]
Since the Ark rested on Ararat?

"I am always ready for the fight —
Let's rise, Æolus, earning glory;
You and I in alliance,
160   Ho ro eile, blow the bellows!"

TR-6

Neptune ri Aeòlus

"Sèid gun aiteal, sèid gun abhsadh,
Sèid le bladadh a ni cnead;
Sèid gu gnuadha, gruamach, gailbheach,
Fuaraidh, fearghasach le fead.

"Sèid gu crosgagach gu 'n dìrich
Marcachd-sìn' os cionn an t-sàil,
Leag do chuip le neart a dh'fhairicheas
Muing is earball nan each bàn.

"Sèid gu cronail, crosda, fiadhaich,
Sèid gun iadhadh, sèid gun tàmh: **170**
Cunbhalach mar mhullach an lìonaidh,
Sèid air ìochdar a' mhuir-tràigh.

"Faraicheam d' anail air na tonnan,
Sèid an doineann gu ceann-fàth,
Air gum fùchd sinn sìos don ghrinneal
Ma tha inneal air an t-snàmh.[10]

"Taisbeanamaid neart mo dhoimhneachd,
Mis', is m' oighreachd aig mo shàil,
Ann an còmhstri nach tèid crìoch air
Fhad 's a bhios a' ghrian gu h-àrd.   **180**

"Sèid gun leasachadh, gun dìobradh,
Sèid da-rìribh, dinn is fàisg;
Sèid mar èirig air do bheatha,
Ged a spreadhadh tu nad chlàir."

TR-6

Neptune to Æolus

"Blow unabated, blow unceasing,
Blow with a great howling sigh;
Blow with fury, gloomy, stormy,
With a chilling, angry whistle.

"Blow up a whirlwind until
Wave-crests rise above the sea,
Crack your whip with force that's felt
By white horses' manes and tails.

"Blow with malice, wild and angry,
170 Blow unswervingly without rest:
Just as strongly as at floodtide,
Blow at the lowest of the ebb.

"Let's feel your breath upon the waves,
Blow up a tempest so that we
Can crush down to the bottom
Any vessel sailing on the sea.

"Let's show the power of my deep,
I, with my followers at heel,
In a battle that will not end
180 So long as sun shines up on high.

"Blow unfailing, unrelenting,
Blow full hard, pound and press;
Blow as if to save your life,
Even if you burst apart."

23

TR-7

Aeòlus ri Neptune

Labhair Aeòlus, " 'S tu mo nàbaidh,
'S tu mo bhràthair san an-uair;
Seasaidh mis' air cùl do shàlach
Is mar as àill leat gheibh thu bhuam.

"Siud mo làmh nach fhàg mi duilleag,
Feur no fionnag a th' air bruaich   **190**
Nach bi dannsadh mullach nan speuran
Nuair a shèideas mise suas.

"'S mòr 's gur uabhasach mo chumhachd
Ann a' spionnadh 's ann a' smuais!
Nì mi blàths a thoirt gu fionnachd
Is nì mi sgiolladh leis an fhuachd.

"Ach an-diugh mo bhòid 's mo mhionnan
Nach eil duine dubh no ruadh
Nach bi gealachadh le aognachd
Nuair a dh'èireas gaoth is cuan.   **200**

"Siud an ceòl as binne leamsa
Na cruit-chiùil a chualas riamh —
Gaoir nam banntraichean 's nam pàistean
Is iad gun àit' am faigh iad dìon.

Æolus to Neptune

Said Æolus, "You are my neighbour,
You are my brother in the storm;
I'll stand hard behind your heels,
All you wish you'll have from me.

"My hand upon it that I'll leave no leaf,
190   Grass-blade or berry on the braes
But will be dancing in the skies above
When my bellows starts to blow.

"Great and awesome is my strength
In vigour and in power!
I can turn warmth to chill
And shell grain with icy blast.

"But today my pledge and vow —
That there is not one, black or brown,
But will be turning pale as death
200   When wind and sea together rise.

"That's sweeter music to my ears
Than any instrument ever heard —
The cries of widows and babes
Without a place to shelter in.

"Làrach lom an àite taighe,
Leac na cagailte 's i fuar,
Mic is athraichean is bràithrean
Brùite, bàtht' air feadh a' chuain.

"Bailtean mòra dol nam fàsach —
Sealladh as àille lem shùil;
Làn de chuirp 's gun duin' air fhàgail
A their àite dhaibh san ùir.

"Garachd an fhithich, gloc na farspaig
Is iad a' sracadh ann an cairbh,
Air an tachdadh leis a' ghionach,
Agus milleanan dhiubh marbh.

"Beanntannan a' dol nam fùirneis
Is iad a' spùtadh teine dearg,
A' sgeith am mionach dhan iarmailt,
A' cnamh 's a' crìonadh 's a' searg.

"Talamh glas a' falbh na luaithre—
Gun an uachdar ach a cheann,
Mis' a' sguabadh lom air aghaidh
Is tus' a' cladhach aig a' bhonn,

"Ga chur an lughad 's an duibhead,
Buaidh is piseach gun robh leinn;
Cuireamaid a-mach à bith e,
'S na biodh nithean ann ach sinn."

210

220

"Bare ruins instead of homes,
Hearthstones dead and cold,
Sons, fathers and brothers
Bruised, drowned in the seas.

"Great cities turned to wasteland —
210   A sight my eyes love to see;
Full of bodies, with no one left
To lay them in the ground.

"Croak of raven, black-back's cry
As they tear at corpses,
Choking with gluttony
As millions lie dead.

"Bens becoming furnaces
As they spout crimson fire,
Spewing their guts to the skies,
220   Crumbling, decaying, consumed.

"Grassland blowing like dust —
Only its surface to be seen —
I sweeping bare the face,
You undermining it beneath.

"In eroding and blackening it,
Victory and success be ours;
Let us destroy its existence,
So there be nothing left but us."

Earrann II

TR-8

Moch-èirigh Phàdraig Mhòir sa mhadainn air an t-siathamh latha deug dhen Mhàrt, 1921.

Dh'èirich Pàdraig moch sa mhadainn,
Ris an leabaidh lùb e ghlùin;   **230**
Thug e adhradh is dh'iarr e beannachd,
Rìgh na Cathrach os a chionn.

Urnaigh dhian le dòchas làidir
Ann an gràdh 's an creideamh beò,
Anns an Trianaid Naomh ag earbsadh,
Ghnìomh ga thairgse chum an glòir.

"Dhuinn ar n-aran làitheil" dh'iarr e,
"Is math ar fiachan dhuinn gu lèir,
Treòrachadh tro Ghleann nan Diar seo
Is beatha shìorraidh às a dhèidh."   **240**

Ann am faosaid a their furtachd
Bhuail e uchd is ghabh e Chreud;
Ghuidh e 'm Freasdal bhith na fhàbhar
Is dh'iarr e còmhnaidh gràsan Dhè.

A dhleasdanas na maidne dèanta —
Tùs a ghnìomh do Dhia nan Dùl —
Sheall e mach gu ceann an taighe
Is ris an adhar thog e shùil.

Movement II

TR-8

Pàdraig Mor rises early on the morning of the 16th March, 1921.[11]

Padraig rose that morning early;
230 Beside the bed he bent his knee,
Said his prayers and asked a blessing
From the King enthroned on high.

Earnest prayer with firm belief
In love and living faith,
In the Holy Trinity trusting,
His work offered for Their glory.

"Give us our daily bread" he prayed,
"And all our trespasses forgive;
Lead us through this Vale of Tears
240 With life eternal after that."

In confession that gives comfort
He beat his breast and said his Creed,
Prayed that Providence might favour him,
Seeking aid from grace of God.

Having made his morning duties —
First of his acts for God above —
He looked out by the gable end
And to the heavens raised his eyes.

Mhuthaich e Bheinn Mhòr fo cleòca,
Buaireas anns na neòil gu h-àrd;   **250**
Bun na gaoithe anns an earra-dheas,
Grian is fearra-ghrian trom a' snàmh.

Chual' e mèilich nan caorach,
'S iad a' sireadh aonach àrd;
Gaoir na geilt' am bial nam faoileag
Is iad nan sgaothan feadh a' bhlàir.

Cha robh tanalach an iar air
Nach robh 'g èirigh fiadhaich àrd;
Eadar Thoile-sgeir is Geò an Dùine
Chunntadh e gach bogha làir.   **260**

Air gach comharra bu lèir dha
Is air na speuran ghabh e beachd,
Is dh'inns a thuigs' air rèir a leughaidh
Gun robh bèistealachd a' teachd.

He noticed Ben More's misty cloak, [12]

250

Turbulence in the clouds on high,
The wind in the south-east quarter,
Sun and mock-sun heavy swimming. [13]

He heard the bleating of the sheep
As they sought a higher ridge;
The seagulls giving anxious cries
As they flocked about the fields.

There was not a shoal to the west
But was rising wild and high;
Between Thoile-sgeir and Geo an Duine [14]

260

He counted every reef exposed.

From each sign that he could see
And from the skies he formed a view;
His judgement told him from his reading
That a monstrous storm was due.

Fhuair e greim air ceirsle shìomain,
Ghreas e chas is gnìomh a làmh;
Sheall e air arbhar 's air iodhlainn,
Dh'acraich e mulain ri làr.

Chuir e fiaragan mun timcheall
Nach biodh iomagain air na sgàth,   270
Ma bha Dia ga fhaicinn iomchaidh
Is gun robh ioma-ghaothach an dàn.

Air am fiaradh is air an tarsainn
Cha robh gainn' air sìomain fraoich,
'S cha robh lùb gun ultach cloiche
Innt' an crochadh air gach taobh.

Chuir e cipeanan san talamh
Is anns na ballachan mun cuairt,
Gus na shaoil leis nach bu bheud dhaibh
Ged a shèideadh na bha shuas.   280

Chuir e fo chlachan an t-àradh,
Lìon e gach càrn is cliabh,
Phut e steach ri fasgadh sgàth iad
Is cùl am màs dhan àird an iar.

Chruinnich e ballain chun na h-àmhthadh,
Thilg e iad air bàrr an t-sùirn;
Dhùin e bhàthaich 's taigh nan capall,
Bior san stapall is taic ri chùl.

He found a clew of heather rope,
Quickened his step and work of hand;
Checked on corn and stackyard,
Anchoring the stacks to the ground.

He put slant lines about them
270   So he would have no fret or fear
If God was to see it fit
That a whirlwind should come.

About them and across them
There was no lack of heather ropes,
Not a loop without its stone
Hanging heavy all around.[15]

He drove tether-pegs into the ground
And into the walls all about,
Until he thought them safe from harm
280   Though the wind should blow its worst.

He weighted the ladder down with stones,
Filled up each sledge and creel,
Pushed them under hurdles' shelter,
Their bottoms facing to the west.

He gathered buckets to the barn,
Threw them on top of the kiln; [16]
He closed the byre and stable,
With staple pins wedged in place.[17]

Bhaganaich e 'n taigh mun mhullach,
Chlach e 'n tubhadh ri bun-baca,   **290**
Dh'ùisnich e cipeannan iarainn
Gus na fiaragan a ghlacadh.

Chuir e cloimhean air gach ursainn
Is dhinn e luideagan gan calcadh;
Dhùin e suas gach toll is uinneag
Is chròidh e tunnagan is cearcan.

Rinn e sgioblachadh gun dàil
Sa h-uile dòigh bu ghnàth leis fhaicinn;
Chaill e roimhid uair no dhà
Le cion 's nach deach e tràth na fhaicill.   **300**

Dh'aithn' e dhaibh gun doras fhosgladh —
"Ma thig crosgag o Ghlaic Ann-Sguir,
Cha bhi againne de dh'fhasgadh
Ach an tobhta - casruisgt', ceannruisgt'.

"Chunnaic mise bliadhna roimhid
Is thug i leatha oirnn am fiar;
Cha do dh'fhàg i bior air balla,
Sop air machair no air sliabh.

"Mas e màirnealaiche mise,
Tha nas miosa tighinn on iar,   **310**
Stoirm nach fhaca mac a rugadh."
Is dìreach mar a thubhairt, b' fhìor.

The house he strengthened round the roof,
290   Weighting thatch to eaves with stones,
He used tether-pegs of iron
To secure the cross-ropes.

He put a latch on every doorpost,
Wedging rags to caulk them tight;
He closed every hole and window
And penned the ducks and hens.

He tidied up without delay
In every usual way he knew;
He lost his way once or twice
300   Through not being early on his guard.

He warned against opening a door —
"If a gust comes from Glaic Ann-Sguir [18]
We will have no more shelter
Than the bare, roofless walls.

"I saw, another year before,
It took with it all our hay,
Leaving not a stick on wall,
No wisp on machair nor on moor.

"If I am any weather-seer,
310   Worse is coming from the west —
Storm no man born has ever seen."
Just as he said, it came to pass.

TR-10

Thàinig dorchadas is ceò,
Dhlùthaich neòil ri talamh glas;
Shaoileadh daoine gun robh ghrian
Air an iarmailt a' dol às.

Shèid i on iar-dheas an uair sin —
'S diocair dhomhsa luadh an rann —
Sgread is fead na gaoithe cruaidhe,
Gaoir nach cuala cluas ach gann.   320

Iorghaill uabhasach nan tonn
Lem bilean crom a-steach gu tràigh,
Osnaich balg-sèididh Aeòluis
Gan toirt beò gu ceòthach bàn.

Dh'èirich suas gach sìlean gainmhich,
Rùisg a' mhealathach chun nan cnàmh,
Caorann is caol-dubh gan spìonadh
As na fhreumhaichean a' sàs.

Cha robh bior air tobhta taighe,
Taobhan no cabar no spàrr,   330
Nach robh falbh aice na fiaclan
Mar gum falbhadh ian le sràbh.

It turned to darkness and mist,
Grey clouds lowered to the ground;
Folk might think that the sun
In the heavens had gone out.

It blew from the south west then —
Hard for me to tell in verse —
The scream and whistle of the gale,
320   A howl the ear has seldom heard.

The awesome tumult of the waves,
Their crests curling into shore,
The blasts from Æolus's bellows
Quickening them to white mist.

There rose up every grain of sand,
The dunes stripped to the bone, [19]
Rowans and black willow torn
Out from their roothold grip.

There was not a timber in a roof,
330   Rafter or beam or spar
But was taken in its teeth
As a bird might snatch a straw. [20]

Chluinnte clachan-moil an aigeil
Ann an aganaidh a' bhàis
Is iad a' bruanadh ris a' chladach,
Air an cagnadh 's air an cnàmh.

Mothar ann am bial gach uamha,
Feadain a' cur suas nan spùt
Is na h-eich bhàna teachd le turtar
Is càch gam pùtadh air an cùl.   **340**

Ri bathais chloiche a' bualadh
'S a' tilleadh le nuallan garbh,
Bùirein aig corrain gan riasladh;
Theich gach iasg a b' urrainn falbh.

Feusgain a' dinneadh an corrag
Anns gach sgàineadh, sgor is eag;
Crith na slige air a' bhàirnich
Is greim a bàis aic' air a' chreig.

38

Shingle of the deep was heard
In the agony of death,
Grinding upon the shore,
Being chewed and eroded.

Thundering in every cave,
Blowholes spouting up
And the white horses crashing in,
340   Driven on by those behind.

Smashing against the rocky face,
Recoiling with a mighty roar;
Thunder of headlands being ravaged;
Every fish that could, escaped.

Mussels tightening their hold
In every crevice, crack or notch;
The limpet trembling in its shell
With a death-grip on the rock.

TR-11

Neptune a' brosnachadh armachd,
A chuip mun earball is mun ceann,   350
'S a chridhe sracadh le farmad:
"Carson a bhiodh Albainn ann?

"Cuim' a dh'fhanainn air mo chrìochan?
Cuim' nach leudaichinn mo ghart?
Cuim' nach buannaichinn an saoghal
Is gun tèid daonnan neart thar cheart?

"Cuim' nach dìrinn chun a' mhullaich?
Cuim' a dh'fhuirichinn nam staid?
A' chlach as ìsle san ursainn,
'S ann oirr' tha 'n cudthrom air fad.   360

"Cuim' nach leanainn prìomh lagh nàdair —
Am fear làidir a thoirt buaidh?
'S ann le càch a chur gu h-ìseal
A gheibh mise dìreadh suas."

Ge b' e dh'èisteadh guth nan tonn,
'S e siud am fonn a bha nam bial
Is iad a' dearbhadh rùn an seanchais,
Mar a dheargadh iad le gnìomh.

Neptune exhorting his armies,
His whip about their heads and tails,
His heart bursting with envy:
"Why should Scotland exist?

"Why stay within my bounds?
Why not widen my estate?
Why not take over the world
When might will always conquer right?

"Why not climb to the very top?
Why should I stay within my place?
It is the threshold's lowest stone
That has to carry all the weight.

"Why not follow Nature's first law —
That the strong will always win?
It is by subduing others
That I will get to climb above."

Whoever listened to the waves
Heard in their voices that refrain
And they proving their words' intent
As they could with their deeds.

350

360

Aeòlus a' sèideadh le dìorras
Glan on iar-dheas oirnn a-steach
Mu chùl nan tonn beucach liatha,
'G èirigh 's a' sìoladh ma seach.

370

Oiteag analach na bèisteadh
Sitir, sèideanach le nuallan;
'S minig an-diugh tha mall gu èirigh,
'S minig tha èisleanach na ghluasad.

Thiormaicheadh i lòin is lodain,
Spìonadh i fodar is fraoch;
Gu ruigeas feusag nan creag
A' falbh le fead aice na craos.

380

Cha robh maid' a bha na sheasamh
Nach do leagadh ris an làr,
Mar a lùbadh lurg a spealgadh
Gus am falbhadh i à sàs.

Chan eil bìdeag bheag a dh'Uibhist
Eadar Uisinnis is Aird Mhaoil,
Eadar Cailtinnis 's an Càrnan
Is gus am fàg thu Taobh a' Chaoil,

Nach do dh'fhàg an là ud sgial ann
Nach tig dìochuimhn' air gu bràth
Is aisigear o bhial gu bial
Mun t-siathamh latha diag dhen Mhàrt.

390

Æolus was fiercely blowing
370   Direct from south-west in on us,
Behind the grey, roaring waves,
Alternately rising and falling.

The gusting breath of the beast
Braying, bellowing, blowing;
Woe betide those late to rise, [21]
Woe betide the slow of foot.

It dried up pools and puddles,
It tore out hay and heather;
Even the moss of the rocks
380   Taken with voracious whistle.

Not a stick that was standing
But was levelled to the ground,
As a splintered stem might bend
Until it falls from its place.

Not the smallest part of Uist
Between Ushinish and Ardvula,
Between Caltinish and Carnan [22]
And until you pass East Kilbride,

But that day left a tale there
390   That will never be forgotten
But will be told from mouth to mouth
About the sixteenth day of March.

boat

Earrann III
TR-12

Mar a thachair do long nan Lochlannach
air a turas-cuain an latha ud agus am
feasgar roimhe agus àireamh bheag mun
luing is mu a sgiobadh.

Thog am bàta o chladach Lochlainn
Feasgar socair, sàmhach, ciùin
Nach gluaiseadh fuiltean air malaidh,
'S an speur gun smal os a cionn.

Bha an ceò bha falbh on fhàirleas
Dol dìreach an-àirde suas;
Cha robh urad slige bhàirnich
Do phlucan air bàrr a' chuain,   **400**

A bha sìtheil, sèimh gun bhuaireas,
Cho soilleir ri fuaran beò
Is cho sleamhainn ri sgàthan glainne,
Fèathail, faileasach, gun deò.

Chìte na craobhan a' fàs ann,
'S am bun ann an àit' an cinn;
Chìte na beanntannan àrd' ann,
'S am mullach an àit' am buinn.

Bha gealach ùr ann am fianais
'S a h-adhaircean fiarach suas;   **410**
Cha robh reult a bh' air an iarmailt
Nach robh ìomhaigh dhith sa chuain.

44

Movement III
TR-12

What befell the Scandinavian ship on her voyage that day and the previous evening, with a little account of the ship and her crew.

The ship left the coast of Norway
On a quiet, calm, peaceful evening
That would not stir a hair on head,
With a cloudless sky above.

The smoke from the galley stack [23]
Climbed straight up on high,
With not so much as a limpet shell
Of ripple on the ocean's face,

That was peaceful, calm, serene,
Limpid as a living spring
And as smooth as a mirror,
Glassy calm without a breeze.

Trees could be seen growing there,
Roots where their tips should be;
The high bens could be seen,
Tops reflected upside-down.

The new moon showed there,
Its curved horns pointing up;
Not a star in the heavens
But had its image in the sea.

A dh'fhacal, bu bhrèagh' an oidhch' i —
Ach bha foill na cridhe dubh;
Cha robh ann ach fèath an Fhaoiltich
Bu ghrad bhiodh a' caochladh cruth.

TR-13

Thàinig oiteag bheag on earra-dheas,
Tuilleadh balbhaidh às a dèidh;
Dh'èirich frionas, friogh is fearghas
Air an fhairge bha cho rèidh.   **420**

Thàinig buaile chruinn mun ghealaich,
Bheòthaich soirbheas, greannach, geur;
Chiar na reultan as an t-sealladh
Ann am falach air an speur.

Chaidh am buachaille gu caoineadh
Is dh'innseadh an glaodh a bha o bheul,
Mu rachadh là eil' a dh'aois air
Gum biodh caochladh air mo sgeul.

Gum faodainn m' fhacal a dhùbladh —
Gum b' e sealladh-sùl' an doill   **430**
A bhith 'g earbs' à madainn gheamhraidh
Gu leanadh i samhla on raoir.

In a word, a lovely evening —
But black treachery in its heart;
It was only a Faoilteach calm [24]
That would quickly change its form.

TR-13

A puff came from the south-east,
With another lull in its wake;
A fretting, angry frown arose
On sea that had been so smooth.

A ring formed around the moon,
A following wind stirred, biting, sharp;
The stars darkened out of sight,
Disappearing in the skies.

The northern loon began to keen [25]
And the sound of its cry foretold
That before it would age a day
There would be a change in my tale.

I could redouble my words —
It would be a blind man's view
To trust that a winter's morning
Would be just like the night before.

420

430

Dh'fhàs i duaichnidh, duathal, dorcha,
Fuar-ghaothach, colgarra, breun,
Eu-coltach an cruth 's an dealbh
Ri feasgar balbh an latha 'n-dè.

Thog an t-aodannan o bathais
Is bho gach athais a bh' air cuan,
Mhionnaich i nach tigeadh rath orr'
Imrich Shathairne no Luan.   440

TR-14

Chuidhticheadh a' long on charraig,
Bha eathar-tarraing ro a sròin
Gu faighte dh'fharsaingeachd cuain i
Gu ionad cur suas nan seòl.

Bu sgaiteach a cuinnean cruadhach,
Bu sgairteil a guaillean àrd
Gu sgapadh is dìreadh chuantan
Le sìnteag uallach om bàrr.

Bodhaig fhada, leathann, bhulgach,
Luchdmhor a dh'fhuilingeadh ri slacraich,   450
Gun deireas buill-bheartadh chruadhach —
Cha robh meang ri luadh na h-acfhainn,

It grew ugly, gloomy, dark
With cold, fierce, turbulent wind,
Quite unlike in shape and form
That quiet evening of yesterday.

The mask slipped from its face
And every omen on the sea
Promised there would be no luck
440   From a Saturday or Monday sailing.

TR-14

The ship was set free from the quay
With a tug under her bow
Till she could be given sea-room
For a place to set her sails.

Sharp was her stem of steel,
Sturdy her tall shoulders
For cleaving and cresting seas,
Leaping proudly from their tops.

A long, broad-bellied hull
450   Capacious to withstand buffeting,
With no lack of steel rigging —
No defect to tell of in her gear.

Teannaichte, ceangailte, suainte,
Ragaichte mun cuairt a beòil
Gu cumail nan crann gun ghluasad,
Diongmhalta, cruaidh nan cuid bhròg.

'S a h-acfhainn ruithe da-rèir sin,
Paisgte rèidh mun cuairt a h-ùrlair;
Bha gach cuibheall, ulag, ailbheag
Air an armadh 's air an ùilleadh.   **460**

Air a ceartachadh na h-uidheam
Bhiodh a slighe righinn searbh,
Gun àite-fasgaidh gu ruitheadh,
'S a ceann-uidhe fad' air falbh.

Bàta làidir, lùthmhor, luaineach,
Astarach air uachdar fairge,
Foghainteach, sliasaideach, guailleach,
Dìonach a dh'fhuaradh 's a dh'fhalbhadh.

Taut, wound and well secured,
Tightened around her gunwale
To keep the masts from moving,
Locked securely in their steps.

In the same way, her running gear
Was folded neatly round her deck;
Each pulley, block and ring-bolt
460   All ready greased and oiled.

For all her sound equipment,
Her voyage would be bitter hard,
With no shelter to run to
And her destination far off.

A strong, sturdy, lively ship,
Swift-moving over the waves,
Stout-quartered and shouldered,
Sound to windward or leeward.

Cha b' e buamastair gun eòlas
A rinn cho bòidheach ri dealbh i   **470**
Ach fear a dh'ionnsaich na òig' e
Mar bu nòs o linn a sheanmhar.

H-uile tarraing leis na dh'fhuaigheadh
Gach cliathach is guala tharbhach,
Thògadh dearg à teine guail i
Ann an càirean cruaidh na teanchair.

Chaidh am barradh 's chaidh am bualadh
Eadar dithis chnuacach, chalma,
Le buillean o chùl an guailleadh
Aig bun Abhainn Chluaidh an Albainn.   **480**

TR-15

Le sgiobadh de ghillean suairce,
Tapaidh, cruadalach, deas, dìreach,
Òga, sgoinneil, ealamh, uallach,
Greimeil, luath-làmhach gu dìreadh

Ri buill chaola, theanna, chruaidhe
Gu ceann fuaraidh na' slat rìoghail;
A chrochadh air ruisg na sùilean,
Ged a chnàmhadh duirn is ìnean.

It was not an unskilled booby
470 Who built her, picture-pretty,
But one who learned while young
Traditions from his granny's time.

Every rivet used to secure
Each side and stout shoulder
Was lifted red-hot from a coal fire
In the steel jaws of the tongs.

They were topped and hammered
Between two strong, skilled men
Striking from above their shoulders
480 At the mouth of Scotland's Clyde.

TR-15

With a crew of fine young lads,
Sturdy, hardy, upstanding,
Youthful, active, nimble, lively,
Sure-handed, quick for climbing

The slender, taut, steel rigging
To windward end of the top-royals;
Who could hang by their eyelashes
Should hands and nails give way.

Do shìol nan reubairean tuathach
Dham bu dualchas cuan is caolas, **490**
Lem birlinnean loma, luatha,
Chothaicheadh iad suas ri aodann

Nan tonn gàireach, greannach, gruamach
Nuair bu chruaidhe fead na gaoithe,
Gun earbs' à inneal gan teàrnadh
Ach an ràmh is neart an gaoirdein.

Sgiobairean fairge gun ghiorag,
Saighdearan smiorail an còmhstri;
Chumadh iad an gnùis ri faobhar
Ged 'iodh fuil is gaorr mum brògan. **500**

Dìorrasach, daingeann air làrach,
Nach do dh'iarr air nàmhaid tròcair,
A' feuchainn ri buille bhualadh
Gus na chuidhtich fuar an deò às.

Càit am bheil eachdraidh ag innse
Sliochd on Fhinn is sìol nan Gàidheal
A bha 'm biùthas àrd air dìreadh
Mun tug Mìlidh às an Spainnt iad?

Seed of the northern pirates
490   Whose heritage was sea and strait,
With their open, swift galleys,
They would confront head on

The roaring, fierce, angry waves
When the wind's howl was loudest,
Trusting no device to save them
But oar and strength of arm.

Sea captains without weakness,
Brave warriors in a fight;
Continuing to face the steel,
500   Wading through blood and gore.

Stubborn, resolute in the field,
Seeking no mercy from the foe;
Still trying to strike a blow
Till the last cold breath had quit.

Where does history record
Descent of the Feinn and seed of Gaels
Who had won high renown
Before Miled brought them out of Spain. [26]

Na fir ainmeil, chalma, chliùiteach
Dham bu dùthchasach a' Ghàidhlig,   **510**
Mu aon a thug bàrr an cruadal
Air na Tuathaich ruadha, bhàna.

Ceatharnach cumadail, calma,
Dìreach, dealbhach air a chnàmhan,
Slinneanach, sliasaideach, calpach,
Nach do sheas fo armaibh àicheadh,

A' spuacadh air sgiath is targaid
Le cuailiche cairgneach, tàirngeach,
Mar choimeas ri buillean sùisteadh
A' slaiceadh air ùrlar àmhthaigh.   **520**

Ged a bhiodh air Neptune mìothlachd,
Dhraghadh iad fheusag gu dàna,
Thilgeadh iad miotag na fhiacail
Is iad ga fhiadhachadh na àite.

Cha leigeadh am misneachd sìos iad
Ged bhiodh iad air bialaibh Shàtain:
Sin mar tha cunntais an gnìomh
A thàinig oirnn o bhial na bàrdachd.

Those celebrated, sturdy men
510   Whose heritage was Gaelic,
        About one who outdid in courage
        The reddish fair-haired Vikings.

        A well-shaped, stout warrior,
        Upright, handsome in his bones,
        Fine shoulders, thighs, calves,
        Brooking no denial under arms.

        Beating dents in shield and targe
        With a knotty, spiked club,
        Like the blows of a flail
520   Thrashing the floor of the barn.

        Even though Neptune be angry,
        They would boldly tweak his beard,
        Throwing a gauntlet in his teeth
        As they challenged him in his domain.

        Their courage would not fail them
        Even if standing before Satan:
        Such is the account of their deeds
        Brought to us from the lips of bards.

Sgaoileadh siùil ri crannaibh àrda,
H-aodach-cinn gu bàrr a spreòd-chruinn,   **530**
Chruaidhicheadh gach cluas dha h-àite
Is ghabh an iùbhrach làn a sgòdaibh.

Curracag ghlas air chùl a sàlach,
Leig i gual' is dh'fhàg i 'n còrsa,
Soirbheas a' sèideadh na sliasaid
'S a h-aghaidh dhan iar fo chòmhdach.

530

Her canvas unfurled on tall masts,
The jib spread to her bowsprit tip;
Each tack hardened in its place
And the tall ship filled her sails.

With a green wake behind her,
She heeled and left the coast,
A fair wind on her quarter,
Heading westward under sail.

Earrann IV

TR-16

Madainn an ath latha

Chiar an oidhche gu glasadh,
Thàinig liathadh an latha
Is cha robh sgeul air ploc fearainn an uair sin;
Cha robh sìon anns an t-sealladh   **540**
A chruthaich Dia air an talamh
A tha fon iarmailt ach farsaingeachd uaine.
Ge b' e taobh air an dearcainn
Cha robh caochladh ri fhaicinn
Ach fairge chaoir-gheal na cearcall mun cuairt dhuinn,
Is ge b' e long air a mìodachd
A bhiodh air meadhan a cìcheadh,
Cha bu mhò i na frìd' air a h-uachdar.

B' e ceann-fàtha na smaointinn
A bhith air ràth ann ad aonar   **550**
Is tu air d' fhàgail air aodann nan cuantan;
Do chuisle phàiteach air traoghadh,
Gun diar ach sàl air gach taobh dhiot,
'S a' ghrian a' deàrrsadh gun fhaochadh a-nuas ort:
Theireadh tìachdadh is claoidh ort
Airson an diar beag a b' fhaoine
Na bha riamh aig do dhaoine chur suarach
Is nach miannach leat fhaotainn
Nì tha miadhail san t-saoghal
Ach do bhial a bhith 'n caochan an fhuarain.   **560**

Movement IV

TR-16

Morning of the next day

Dark night turned to grey,
The light of dawn broke
With not a trace of land now to be seen;
540   There was nothing in sight
That God created on earth
Under heaven but a vast spread of green.
Whichever way I looked
Nothing else could be seen
But foaming sea circled about;
Even the biggest of ships
In the midst of its swells
Would be no more than a mite on its face.

It would be a subject for thought
550   To be on a raft all alone,
Abandoned on the face of the sea;
Your thirsty veins drained,
Nothing but brine all around,
No relief from the sun burning down.
Thirst and weakness would compel you,
For sake of the tiniest drop,
To care nothing for all family wealth;
You would not wish to have
Anything prized by the world
560   But your lips at the fount of a spring.

TR-17

Ach, a thionndadh rim sgiala,
Thromaich gnùise na h-iarmailt,
Dh'fhàs i dubh-ghorm, iargalta, gruamach,
Craobh na lùban on iar-aird
A' falbh nan stiùpannan stiallach,
Bu domhainn, dùmhail a' ghrian ann am buaile.
Cha robh feum air fear màirneil
A dhèanadh fiosachd no fàisneachd
Mun tigeadh a-màireach mun cuairt oirnn;
Thuig gach duine den chòmhlan   570
Is leubh iad soilleir sna neòil e -
Gum biodh Neptune is Aeòlus air ghluasad.

Dh'fhas a' ghaoth na bu ghèire
Is chaidh a' ghailleann gu sèideadh
Is chaidh an fhairge na sèisdear le nuallan;
Bha i casadh a drèineadh,
A' tighinn a-steach thar na slèisne
'S a' ruith cho bras ri each-rèise tro gualainn;
Gillean smearala, trèine
Sìor thoirt sanas dha chèile,   580
'S gann gu' cluinneadh iad eubha nan cluasan,
Ri buill a phasgadh 's a rèiteach
Is nach seas iad cas ach air èiginn,
'S ise a' laighe 's ag èirigh 's a' suainteadh.

But, to return to my tale,
The face of the heavens turned dark,
It grew blue-black, turbulent, angry;
Clouds eddied from the west,
Streaming in ragged trails,
The sun in a halo deep-smothered.
There was no need of a seer
Who could foretell or predict
Before the morrow came round;
570   Each one of the crew understood
And read it clear in the clouds –
Neptune and Æolus would be stirring.

The wind cut ever keener,
The gale started to blow;
The sea set siege with a roar,
Looking ever more ugly,
Pouring in over her quarters,
At racehorse speed through her scuppers;
Courageous, strong lads
580   Ever encouraging each other,
Hardly hearing a shout in their ears,
Neatly stowing the halyards,
Though they could scarce keep their feet
As she pitched and she tossed and she rolled.

A' tighinn an tòir air an t-soitheach
Gun tàinig Aeòlus na b' aghaiche,
Muir air tòcadh 's i cladhach 's a ruamhar,
Ag èirigh cròiceach mar coinneamh,
Cho gile sròn ris a' choinneal
A' tighinn mu spreòd-chrann na goilleanan uaine: **590**
Bha h-uile seòl ann an lughadh,
'S a h-uile òirleach dhiubh draghadh
Is bha ise falbh mar a stadhadh i 'n uair sin
'S i dol ri fairge le faghar
Le togail fhalbhanach adhartach,
Mar an earba 's an fhaghaid ga ruagadh.

A h-uile gleadhar dhe cliathaich,
'S a h-uile sloc theid i sìos ann,
Gun toir i boc air a fiaradh a-nuas às;
I gabhail chnoc air am fiacail   **600**
Is i ga' sgoltadh is ga' stialladh
Mar thèid an coltar tron fhiadhaire luachrach:
Muir ag èirigh dhan iarmailt,
A mhullach nan speuran na siaban
Mar ionnan 's sèideag an grìosach na luaithre,
'S a h-uile h-alt innte dìosgan,
A' sgonnadh chnapan o sliasaidean
Mar gun sgapadh na diasan fon bhuailtean.

In hot pursuit of the vessel
Æolus became ever bolder,
Swelling seas probing and delving;
Rising raging before us
With crests candle-white,
Boiling green right over her bowsprit:
Every sail was reefed in,
Every inch of them pulling
And she then going at full stretch,
Crashing through the waves
With a leaping, forward movement
Like the roe deer chased by the hunt.

Every crash on her side,
Every trough she sinks down in,
She leaps up again, heeling over;
Taking swells in their teeth
Cleaving and tearing
As ploughshare cuts rushy moorland:
Seas rising up to the skies,
To the roof of the heavens in spray
Like ash blown up from the embers;
Every joint in her creaking,
Shedding showers from her quarters
As grain scatters under the flail.

TR-18

Thàinig Aeòlus gu crosdachd,
Chruinnich e thuige na h-osnaidh;   610
Sheas e daingeann is dh'fhosgail e luamha,
Fhuair e sgamhan a lìonadh,
Ghabh e cuimis oirr' on iar-dheas
Is leig e mach na bha shìos de chuis-uabhais.
Chaidh an iùbhrach gu siabadh,
A' laighe nunn air a cliathaich
Is cha toir stiùir air a fiaradh a-nuas i:
"Suas sibh, 'illean, gu làidir;
Glacaibh calpannan tairgne;
Thoiribh dhith na siùil àrda, tha 'n uair ann."   620

Leigeadh leath' a cuid sgòdaibh,
Chluint' i crathadh a còmhdaich,
Chìte fallas a' còpadh le gruaidhean,
'S a cuid lasgairean òga,
Gun fon casan ach ròpa,
Dol an caraibh nan seòl gan toirt bhuaipe;
Ris na slatan ga' fùcadh,
Gan cumail aca le rùdain,
'S an ròpa gasgain is lùb is snaoim cruaidh air:
Hò-rò-gheallaidh is ùpraid,   630
'S i dol o smachd air an stiùir orra,
Cumail cagnadh ri triùir ac' a' tuairneadh.

Æolus turned to fury,
610   Gathered the gusts to him,
Stood firm and opened his throat;
Having filled his lungs,
He took aim from south-west
And released all of his terrible power.
The vessel was swept away,
Lying over on her beam-ends,
The rudder's angle cannot bring her to:
"Up you go, lads, strongly;
Take hold of the halyards —
620   Reef in the topsails — it is time."

Her sails were let go,
Her canvas heard flapping,
Sweat seen pouring from brows,
As her strapping young men,
With but rope for a foothold,
Got to grips with furling her sails;
Folding them to the yards,
Holding them down with their knuckles
With the tie-rope knotted and hitched:
630   Uproar and confusion
As she fails to answer her helm,
Keeping three at work turning the wheel.

Ged a bheagadh a h-aodach
Cha do sheas i ach slaodach
Is cha do leasaich air saothair nan Tuathach:
Bha i 'n geall air a taomadh
Is leis na fhuair i do thaosgnadh,
I air thuar a bhith sgaoilt' anns na fuaigheil.
Bha 'n crann-toisich le cliathaich,
'S a chuid acfhainn na h-iallan   **640**
Is nuair a sgaradh an driamlach sin bhuaipe,
Sruth dhen fhuil às am meòirean
A' ruitheadh gibean do sheòl oirre,
Feuch an tigeadh a sròn chun an fhuaraidh,

Labhair Neptune ri Aeòlus
"Tha 'n crann-toisich na òirnean,
Lagaidh sin iad nan dòchas, tha bhuaidh leinn!
Tha i nist againn leònta,
Siud air n-adhart sinn còmhla
Is cha tig ise gu còrsa le luathair.   **650**
Thoir gach sibheag dhe còmhdach
Leat na ribeagan ròineach
Is fàgaidh mise gach bòrd dhith na' fuairnean:
Cha dèan misneachd no eòlas
A toirt a-nist às mo chrògan
Is na biodh snìom a gheibh tròcaire bhuainne.

Though her sails were reefed in
She handled but poorly
And the work was no less for the Norsemen:
She was in sore need of pumping
As from all the rough handling
She was in danger of spreading her seams.
The foremast over the side,
640   Its rigging in shreds,
And, with all of that tangle cut free,
Their fingers streamed blood
Running up a rag of a sail
So her head might come round into wind.

Neptune said to Æolus:
"The foremast is splintered -
That will weaken their hopes, we have won!
We have her now stricken,
Let us go forward together
650   And she will never make speed to shore.
Take every shred of her canvas
With you in tatters away
And I'll shatter each one of her planks;
Neither courage nor skill
Will get her now from my clutches,
Let no distress receive mercy from us."

Chaidh a' ghailleann gu bùirich, [27]
Chaidh an fhairge gu fùistneadh
Is chaidh a' charachd air iùbhrach nan Tuathach;
Bha i glact' air a cùlaibh,   660
'S a cuid shlatan gun tionndadh
Is cha robh maid' os a cionn nach do sguabadh.
Chaidh a sgiobadh fo mhùiseag,
Thuit an cridhe gu 'n glùinean
Nuair a chunnaic iad rùisgt' air a' chuan i,
'S iad gun chomas a teàrnadh:
"Cò bheir cobhair nar càs dhuinn?"
Chaidh an achanaigh àraid seo suas leo:

TR-19

"Fhir a chruthaich an tùs sinn,
A th' air cathair nan dùilean   670
Is ris na peacaich nach diùlt a bhith truasail,
Leig le fàthmas Do shùil oirnn
A th' ann an gàbhadh na cunntais
Le dhol ad lathair gun iompadh, gun fhuasgladh.
Eist gu grad ri ar n-ùrnaigh
Tha dol nar n-airce gad ionnsaigh
Is ged a thoill sinn Do dhìombadh, thoir cluas dhi;
Air sgàth Do charthantachd dhùinne [28]
A rinn le droigheann Do chrùnadh;
Thoir gu cala is gu ciùineachd na Tuathaich."   680

The storm turned to a bellow,
The sea turned to raging,
The tall Norse ship was heeled over;
660   She was taken aback
Before her yards could be turned
And every stick above deck swept away.
Her crew were dismayed,
Their hearts down in their boots,
When they saw her bare-decked on the sea
With no power to rescue her now,
"In hour of need who will save us?"
They offered this desperate prayer:

TR-19

"O One who first made us,
670   Who sits on the elements' throne,
And refuses not mercy to sinners,
Look down to reprieve us
At risk of our reckoning
Without conversion or absolution before You.
Hear quickly our prayer
Who in distress approach You,
Though we deserve your displeasure, give it heed;
For the sake of your love for us
Who crowned you with thorns,
680   Bring the Norsemen to harbour and peace."

"Thus', a Phrionnsa na Sìthe,
Dhuinne 's Ughdar is Cìobair,
Fhir a dhùraig a' chìs a bh' oirnn fhuasgladh,
Fhir as Buachaille dìleas
A tha D' uain Agad prìseil,
A tha gan cuallach air fìor-uisg' an fhuarain;
Fhir a shàbhail 's a shaor sinn,
Fhir a cheannaich gu daor sinn,
Fhir thug mathanas saor iomadh uair dhuinn,
Cuir an t-srian ris na cìdhlean   **690**
Aig na siantannan millteach
Is ann Ad mhìorbhailtean ìslich an uabhar."

"Eist, a Chrìosda, rim achanaigh,
Cuimhnich diadhachd ar n-athraichean
Bhon as Triath Thu 's as caraide buan dhuinn,
A rinn gu piantail ar n-anam
Bho ifreann ìochdraich a cheannach,
'S a gheall san t-sìorraidheachd flathanas shuas dhuinn:
Air Do mhìothlachd is airidh sinn
Le bhith sìor dhol o D' rathaidean,   **700**
Ach, a Thìghearna, thig mathanas Bhuatsa;
Is seall air daoine th' air allaban,
Rèitich aodann na mara dhuinn
Is caisg am Faoilteach 's an Gearran 's an Sguabag."

"O You, Prince of Peace,
Our Ruler and Keeper,
One who wished to free us from sin,
One who is faithful Shepherd
Who holds Your lambs precious,
Tending them with pure spring water;
One who saved and delivered us,
One who redeemed us so dearly,
One who forgave us freely so often,
690   Put a curb on the jaws
Of the destructive elements,
In Your miracles, lessen the terror."

"Listen, O Christ, to my prayer,
Remember the faith of our fathers,
As You are Lord and eternal friend to us,
Who, through suffering, redeemed
Our souls from hell down below
And promised us heaven eternal above:
We deserve Your displeasure,
700   Ever forsaking Your ways,
But, Lord, forgiveness comes from You;
Look down on those who are lost,
Calm the face of the sea for us,
Curb the Wolfwind, Cutter and Sweeper."[29]

TR-20

Labhair Neptune ri Aeòlus,
"Ma tha Esan gan còmhnadh,
Thèid an latha seo oirnne, mo thruaighe!
Ged bhiodh sàl innte dòrtadh
Gu 'm biodh i làn chun a' bheòil dheth,
Cumaidh Esan, mas deòin Leis, i 'n uachdar: 710
'S bochd is gur dorranach dhòmhsa
Gu bheil i ruith tro mo mheòirean
Is gun mi ceathramh na h-òirlich o bhuannachd;
Ach, o 's Esan an t-Ughdar,
Chan eil seasamh tro ghnùis dhuinn
 Is feumaidh sinne le ùmhlachd toirt suas Dha."

A' Chrìoch

74

Said Neptune to Æolus,
"If He comes to their aid
The day goes against us, alas!
Though salt sea should pour into her
Till she fills to the gunwales,
710   Should He choose, He can keep her afloat:
It's bitter disappointment for me
That she slips through my fingers
When not a quarter-inch from success;
But, as He is the Ruler,
We have no standing before Him
And humbly we are forced to submit".

The End

Notes

1. Hermes (Greek) or Mercury (Roman) – the messenger of the gods.

2. Homer (9th Century BC) – Credited as author of the ancient Greek epic poems *Iliad* (dealing with the Trojan War) and *Odyssey* (Odysseus's adventures on his voyage home).

3. The *Feinn* were the followers of Fingal *Fionn Mac Cumhail*, whose exploits are celebrated in the Ossianic heroic ballads (believed by some authorities to date from the 8th Century AD). They were summoned to battle by Fingal's horn known as the *Còrn Fiùdha*. Legend has it that they still sleep in a cave where an unwary traveller once stumbled upon them. He found the horn and blew a blast upon it which caused them to stir. At a second blast they rose to rest on their elbows, which caused the terrified visitor to flee – leaving them to complain that he left them less comfortable than he found them!

4. *Dorraraich* – more usually spelt *dairirich* or *dairireach*. The bard varied the spelling of this onomatopoeic word to provide the required internal rhyme with *stoirm*. (See notes 7 & 27).

5. *Deigheann* – literally a shackle for a horse.

6. The Rock of Nicholson's Leap (close by the eastern shore of South Uist behind Hecla) is so-called because legend has it that the gap was leapt by the eponymous Nicholson to escape pursuing Clanranald's men.

7. The ms had *Scòidh*, which could not be located. However, the Howmore map in the Ordnance Survey 1:25,000 series (revised 1976) shows *Uamh Dubh na Sgogaich* near Uishinish lighthouse about 2 km. north of Nicholson's Leap

(see above). OS Gaelic names are sometimes unreliable so it is possible that this is a corruption of the original. An example of the local pronunciation encountered suggested the spelling should be *Sgothaidh* (of the boat). The rhyme scheme requires assonance with *sgòrnan* and the fact that Macintyre had added a (rare!) accent in the ms suggests the rules of rhyme should take precedence over accuracy. Even the most skilled bards would bend rules occasionally in the interest of rhyme. (See note 27.)

8. *Traigh Bhàn* is the name given to a stretch of machair at Ormiclate which presumably was once a loch or bay of the sea and is now filled in. It is still boggy in wet conditions. It has not been possible to identify precise locations for *Mol nan Dòrnag*. However, the pebble shingle bays north and south of the Uisinish headland are known as the *Mol a Tuath* and the *Mol a Deas* respectively.

9. See Note 4.

10. This verse from the ms was not included in the published version in *Sporan Dhòmhnaill*.

11. Patrick MacDonald, *Pàdraig mac Dhòmhnaill 'ic Fhearghais 'ic Phàdraig,* was a real person who lived in Milton close to the main road.

12. Ben More (literally 'Big Mountain') is the highest of the Uist hills. Its old name was *Gèideabhal* (cf. Goatfell in Arran) and its southern (higher) peak is *Buail' a' Ghoill*.

13. *Fearra-ghrian* – mock-sun — a bright spot caused by diffraction of light through ice crystals in clouds.

14. *Thoilesgeir* is the lenited spelling in the ms. but the rocks shown on the Kildonan shore on the Daliburgh Map 201 of the OS 1:25,000 Pathfinder series (revised 1976) are marked

Trollaskeir. This agrees with the Gaelic pronunciation of Neil Macmillan of Milton. *Geò an Dùine* is the small bay south of Ardvula point next to the ruins of an ancient fort.

15. Heavy stones were used to secure the ties on corn and hay stacks as well as the thatch of houses.

16. The old barns would have a kiln for drying the grain prior to milling. As the bard makes clear at line 520, the Uist word for barn was *àmhthaigh* (literally kiln-house). In the supplement to *Gaelic Words and Expressions from South Uist and Eriskay* Fr. Allan McDonaldgives *àmhthaidh* as the dative of kiln, emphasising that the h sound is clearly heard before the final vowel. The ms has the variation at line 285, presumably for assonance

17. The latch would have a simple eye fitting over a staple with a tapered peg (often wooden) through the staple to hold it in place.

18. *Glac Ann-Sguir* is on the western flanks of Ben More (see Note 12).

19. *Mealathach* or *mealbhach* – 'a stretch of machair with bent-covered hillocks' — according to Fr. Allan McDonald's *Gaelic Words and Expressions from South Uist and Eriskay*. A stretch of the Askernish machair is so-called.

20. A house near to the bard's birthplace in Snishival had its thatched roof blown away in the 1921 storm. Although his family had moved to Kildonan by then, this may have been part of the original inspiration.

21. *Minig* (l. 375) is used in Uist rather than *mairg* as in other areas.

22. Caltinish is a headland on the northeast of South Uist

approached via the Loch Carnan road while *Taobh a' Chaolais* (literally "Beside the Sound") is the Gaelic name for East Kilbride in the south of the island. Ushinish and Ardvula are headlands on the east and west of the island respectively.

23. *Fàirleas* was usually used for the hole made in the roof of the old thatched houses to allow the smoke to escape.

24. The current Gaelic names for the months are of relatively recent coinage. Although *Faoilteach* is now used for January it was originally a much later and more loosely defined period in late January or February. According to Dwelly, it might also refer to the spring equinox — which would be appropriate in this case.

25. The Gaelic line is thus in the ms. In *Sporan Dhòmhnaill* (edited by the Rev. Somerled Macmillan) it was changed to *Chaidh 'm buna-bhuachaille gu caoineadh* — perhaps in the interest of clarity.

26. *Milidh* – according to legend the Celts came to Ireland via Egypt, Crete and Spain. Their leader was Miled or Milesius whose wife was a Pharaoh's daughter named Scota. He himself died in Spain but his sons Eber and Eremon defeated the Dé Danann and eventually divided Ireland up between themselves.

27. The ms has *an gailleann* – perhaps for better assonance with *an fhairge*.

28. The ms has a grave accent on the *'u'* — as required by the rhyme scheme at this point. As DR used accents very rarely, this is presumably another example of the lengthening of a short vowel. (See note 7).

29. Three periods associated with winter gales. (See note 23).

GRACE NOTE PUBLICATIONS Ltd is committed to publishing works in Gaelic and Scots to support the conservation of Scottish culture.

Tha **GRACE NOTE PUBLICATIONS Ltd** fo ghealltanas leabhraichean fhoillseachadh sa Ghàidhlig is an Albais mar thaic gus cultar na h-Alba a ghleidheadh.

For more information and catalogue request contact:
Grace Note Publications
Grange of Locherlour
Ochtertyre by Crieff
Perthshire PH7 4JS
Scotland

Tel: +44 (0) 1764 655 979
E-mail: books@gracenotereading.co.uk

Postage and packing is free within UK. For overseas orders, postage and packing (airmail) will be charged at 30% of the total order value.

Grace Note
Publications